ONE THOUSAND THINGS WORTH KNOWING

tems should be returned on or before the last date
shown below. Items not already requested by other
borrowers may be renewed in person, in writing or by
telephone. To renew, please quote the number on the
barcode label. To renew online a PIN is required.
This can be requested at your local library.
Renew online @ **www.dublincitypubliclibraries.ie**
Fines charged for overdue items will include postage
incurred in recovery. Damage to or loss of items will
be charged to the borrower.

Leabharlanna Poiblí Chathair Bhaile Átha Cliath
Dublin City Public Libraries

Date Due	Date Due	Date Due
0 2 MAR 2015		
2 5 MAR 2015		
0 2 AUG 2016		
0 8 DEC 2017		

ONE THOUSAND THINGS
WORTH KNOWING

PAUL MULDOON

FABER & FABER

First published in 2015 by
Faber & Faber Ltd
Bloomsbury House
74–77 Great Russell Street
London WC1B 3DA

A CIP record for this book is available from the British Library

ISBN 978–0–571–31604–5

2 4 6 8 10 9 7 5 3 1

CONTENTS

ONE THOUSAND THINGS WORTH KNOWING

CUTHBERT AND THE OTTERS

In memory of Seamus Heaney

Notwithstanding the fact that one of them has gnawed a strip
    of flesh
from the shoulder of the salmon,
relieving it of a little darne,
the fish these six otters would fain
carry over the sandstone limen
and into Cuthbert's cell, a fish garlanded with bay leaves
and laid out on a linden flitch

like a hauberked warrior laid out on his shield,
may yet be thought of as whole.
An entire fish for an abbot's supper.
It's true they've yet to develop the turnip clamp
and the sword with a weighted pommel
but the Danes are already dyeing everything beige.
In anticipation, perhaps, of the carpet and mustard factories

built on ground first broken by the Brigantes.
The Benedictines still love a bit of banter
along with the Beatitudes. Blessed is the trundle bed,

it readies us for the tunnel

from Spital Tongues to the staithes. I'm at once full of dread

and in complete denial.

I cannot thole the thought of Seamus Heaney dead.

In the way that 9 and 3 are a perfect match

an Irish war band has 27 members.

In Barrow-in-Furness a shipyard man scans a wall for a striking
    wrench

as a child might mooch

for blackberries in a ditch. In times to come the hydrangea

will mark most edges of empire.

For the moment I'm hemmed in every bit as much

by sorrow as by the crush of cattle

along the back roads from Durham to Desertmartin.

Diseart meaning "a hermitage."

In Ballynahone Bog they're piling still more turf in a cart.

It seems one manifestation of the midge

may have no mouthparts.

Heartsore yet oddly heartened,

I've watched these six otters make their regal

progress across the threshold. I see how they might balk

at their burden. A striped sail

will often take years to make. They wear wolf or bear pelts,
the berserkers. Like the Oracle
at Delphi, whose three-legged stool
straddles a fiery trough

amid the still-fuming heaps of slag,
they're almost certainly on drugs. Perhaps a Viking sail handler,
himself threatened with being overwhelmed,
will have gone out on a limb and invented a wind tiller
by lashing a vane to the helm?
That a longship has been overturned on the moor
is as much as we may surmise

of a beehive cell thrown up along the Tyne.
The wax moth lives in a beehive proper. It can detect sound
frequencies up to 300 kHz. The horse in the stable
may be trained to follow a scent.
What looks like a growth of stubble
has to do with the chin drying out. I straighten my
black tie as the pallbearer

who almost certainly filched
that strip of skin draws level with me. Did I say "calamine"?
I meant "chamomile." For the tearoom nearest to Grizedale Tarn
it's best to follow the peat stain

of Grizedale Beck. A prototype of backgammon
was played by the Danes. Even Mozart would resort to a recitative
for moving things along. Halfway through what's dissolved into
    the village

of Bellaghy, this otter steps out from under the bier
and offers me his spot. It seems even an otter may subordinate
himself whilst being first in line to revolt.
He may be at once complete insider and odd man out.
Columbanus is said to have tamed a bear
and harnessed it to a plow. Bach. The sarabande.
Under the floor of Cuthbert's cell they've buried the skull of a colt

born with a curvature of the spine.
Even now we throw down a challenge like a keel
whilst refraining from eating peach pits for fear of cyanide.
Refrain as in *frenum*, "a bridle."
We notice how a hook on the hind wing of a moth
connects it to an eye on the forewing. A complex joint
if ever there was one. According to our tanners,

the preservation of hides involves throwing caution
to the wind. Their work permits
allowed Vikings to sack Armagh in 832. The orange

twine helps us keep things straight. I once sustained concussion,
having been hit by a boom in Greenwich,
and saw three interlocking red triangles on my beer mat.
The way to preserve a hide is not by working into it Irish moss
    or casein

but the very brains
of the very beast that was erstwhile so comfortable in its skin.
Irish monasticism may well derive from Egypt.
We don't discount the doings of the Desert Fox
any more than Lily Langtry's shenanigans with Prince
Louis of Battenberg. The 1920s vogue for sequins
began with Tutankhamen. Five wise virgins

are no more likely than five foolish
to trim a fish-oil lamp to illumine
the process of Benedictine nuns spinning and weaving yarns.
I don't suppose we'll ever get to grips with the bane
of so many scholars—the word *SINIMIAINIAIS*
inscribed on a Viking sword. As for actually learning to grieve,
it seems to be a nonstarter. The floor of Cuthbert's cell is flush

with the floor of Ballynahone Bog after the first autumn rains,
the gantries, the Woodbines, the drop scones,

the overflowing basin's chipped
enamel, the earth's old ointment box, the collop of lox,
the drumroll of wrens
at which we still tend to look askance.
This style of nasal helmet was developed by the Phrygians

while they were stationed at Castledawson.
The barrow at Belas Knap was built before the pyramids.
Same thing with Newgrange.
The original seven-branched menorah's based on a design
by Moses himself. When it comes to the crunch
we can always fall back on potassium bromide
as an anticonvulsant. A chamomile tisane

in a tearoom near the Bigrigg iron mine.
Since the best swords are still made from imported steel,
the more literal among us can't abide
the thought an island may be tidal.
This is the same Cuthbert whose chalice cloth
will be carried into battle on the point
of a spear. I can just about visualize a banner

of half-digested fish fluttering through the air
from the otter spraint

piled high at the threshold of Cuthbert's dry stone holt.
A sea trout is, after all, merely a brown trout
with wanderlust. It wears a tonsure from ear to ear
like any Irish aspirant.
We'll still use the term "smolt"

of a salmon that first leaves fresh water for salt. Vikings will fletch
their arrows with goose long into the era of Suleiman
the Magnificent. A tithe barn
often cedes another tenth of its grain.
We won't have been the first to examine
our consciences at Bishop's Cleeve.
Benedictine monks will extend their tradition of persiflage

far beyond the confines
of Northumbria. Long after the Synod
of Whitby has determined the penis bone of an otter may double
as a tiepin. A grave's best filled with Lough Neagh sand.
We use a guideline when we dibble
cauliflower plants so things won't go awry.
A calcium carbide "gun" still does duty as a pigeon-scarer

in the parish of Banagher, a parish where a stag
has been known to carry in its antlers

a missal, a missal from which a saint might pronounce.
Let's not confuse candelabras with chandeliers.
I'd as lief an ounce
of prevention as a pound of cure,
particularly when it comes to the demise

of a great skald. Coffin is to truckle
as salmon is to catafalque.
Could it be that both the trousers *and* the coat of mail
were invented by the Celts?
It's no time since Antrim and Argyll
were under Áedán mac Gabráin's rule.
We come together again in the hope of staving off

our pangs of grief. An altar cloth carried into battle
by the 82nd Airborne. A carton
of Lucky Strikes clutched by a G.I. on the bridge
at Toome. I want to step in to play my part
while the sky above the hermitage
does a flip chart.
Gray, blue, gray, blue, gray. However spartan

his beehive hut, Cuthbert has developed a niche
market in fur, honey, amber,

and the sweet wine we'll come to know as Rhenish.
Sometimes it takes only a nudge
to start a longship down a trench.
In 832, by most tallies, the Vikings did a number
on Armagh not once but thrice. I want that coffin to cut a notch

in my clavicle. Be they "lace curtain" or "shanty,"
Irish Americans still hold a dirge chanter
in the highest esteem. That, and to stand in an otter's stead.
The chiastic structure of the book of Daniel
mimics a double ax-head.
As with the stubble, so with the finger- and toenails.
I cannot thole the thought of Seamus Heaney dead.

In South Derry as in the coalfields of South Shields
a salmon has been known to dance along a chariot pole.
In the way we swap "scuttle" for "scupper"
we're flummoxed as much by the insidiousness of firedamp
as our sneaking regard for Rommel.
I think of an otter cortege
passing under a colonnade of fig trees

barren despite their show of foliage.
We know neither the day nor the hour of our summons.

The same Cuthbert of Lindisfarne

whose body will be carried aloft by monks fleeing those same
Danes.

Mountbatten of Burma. Montgomery of Alamein.

All with the same insignia on their scale-armored sleeves.

Refulgent all. From *fulgere*, "to flash."

PELT

Now rain rattled
the roof of my car
like holy water
on a coffin lid,
holy water and mud
landing with a thud

though as I listened
the uproar
faded to the stoniest
of silences . . . They piled
it on all day
till I gave way

to a contentment
I'd not felt in years,
not since that winter
I'd worn the world
against my skin,
worn it fur side in.

CHARLES ÉMILE JACQUE:
POULTRY AMONG TREES

It was in Eglish that my father kept the shop
jam-packed with Inglis loaves, butter,
Fray Bentos corned beef, Omo, Daz, Beechams Powders,
Andrews liver salts, Halls cough drops,

where I wheezed longingly from my goose-downed truckle
at a Paris bun's sugared top.
A tiny bell rang sweetly. The word on the tip
of my tongue was "honeysuckle."

When one of his deep-litter chickens filled its crop
with hay from the adjoining shed
my father opened it with a razor blade, reached
in, pulled out the shimmering sop,

then sewed it up with a darning needle and thread.
That childhood memory came back
now a fracas had left two hens with gaping beaks,
one with what seemed a severed head.

Though I might have taken the blueprint of a shack
from *Poultry Keeping for Dummies,*
I'd fancied myself more an Ovid in Tomis—
determined to wing it, to tack

together Jahangiri Mahal from a jumble
of 2×4 studs, malachite,
run-of-the-mill planks, cedar shingles, more offcuts
in New Jersey's rough-and-tumble.

Now it looked as if there had been a pillow fight
in and around the chicken run.
Our pointer, Sherlock, had instigated a reign
of terror, scaring the daylights

out of the hens (in a spirit of good clean fun,
no doubt), launching a morning raid
such as Meleager & Co. had launched to root
out the great boar of Calydon.

Their temperature being 106 centigrade
might account for the quizzical
view chickens take of history going in cycles,
but I could divine from the jade

of her exposed neck, the movement of her gizzard
jewelled by broken oyster shells,
one hen had ventured so far on the gravel shoals
she'd become less hen than lizard.

As the echoes of Sherlock's high-pitched rebel yells
clung to the thatch in a smoke knot,
I'd only very gradually taken note
how Herbert Hoover's casting spells

(and offering that "chicken in every pot")
had come too late for Robert Frost,
cooped up as he'd been on the edge of a forest
with some 300 Wyandottes.

Odd that the less obviously wounded hen be lost
to the great realm of the cageless
while a slash-throat somehow lingers. Though I cudgeled
my brains, the only thought that crossed

my mind was how the sisters of Meleager
had once morphed into guinea hens.
I found myself looking to Aries, the heinous
Dog Star, then to Ursa Major.

Those next few days, the slash-throat held out a quill pen
with which we might together draw
up a plan for how I could help her muddle through.
Her comb and wattles were cayenne

under a heat lamp. Her throat left my own throat raw.
She lifted her head on its latch.
It was as if a sop of hay had become lodged
in my own mother-of-pearled craw.

The ears of barley, whole wheat, and corn mixed from scratch
I boiled down further. My new razor
had me on edge. I was such an early riser
I'd become less man than rooster. An extra batch

of the barley/wheat/corn mush might help her brazen
it out. Till she could shake a leg
(and a wing!), I'd feed her the stuff I myself like—
marigolds, cottage cheese, raisins.

Though Fabergé's first inlaying a gilt hen egg
was by imperial decree
it's easy to see why we dunghill roosters crow
when we set off a powder keg

at our own behest, winding ourselves with a key
till our workaday art's a match
for workaday life, a feature rarely as much
to the fore as in *Poultry Among Trees*.

Here the angle of the ridgepole (though blurred by thatch)
leads the eye to an odd focal
point where two hen harriers confirm how fickle
is our grasp on things. If a patched

chicken did once attest to his skill in sewing,
my father still boned up in full
on "how to remove the merry-thought of a fowl"
from *One Thousand Things Worth Knowing*.

Even if I have helped my own hen to pull
through by dint of mash and mush-talk
I'm still far less disposed to look to the sky dog
for assent, or to the sky bull,

to look to any of those old cocks-of-the-walk.
Not for me strutting out at dusk
and pretending to be equal to any task
while sporting a cayenne Mohawk.

Once I glimpsed the ideal under a dry husk.
All I see now is the foible
in a sword. I often think of Aesop's fable
where a great boar sharpens his tusk

against all likelihood. Now being a goitered
rooster is all that's on the cards
for me, I suspect, consigned to the pile of grit
I myself once reconnoitered.

I was a Rhode Island Red rooster standing guard
in Eglish as my father sliced.
"Think like a man of action," wrote Mr. Sallust,
"act like a man of thought." The yard

opened on my less-than-steady Peter, then Christ,
then the rum-numbed hen, then the nail
from which it hung. As an emblem of renewal,
surely that hen would have sufficed?

My own new regimen of cottage cheese and kale
continues to help me toughen
my resolve in ways Sherlock himself might divine.
The elongation of his tail

has been traced to a long line of partridge flushers
and catchers of hares on the hop.
I don't mind being relegated to the heap
where I once stood as both door and usher.

For I've no aspirations now ever to strop
my beak on the bark of a church.
Ever to be a weather vane . . . To be in charge . . .
That's for a motorcycle cop,

all Ray-Bans and chrome, so ill at ease on the perch
of a fire escape in a flop-
house in west L.A., the downy feathers he'll flip
through in a routine background search.

Now my right-as-rain hen, like my father's post-op
hen, will shine out from her dunghill.
That sweet little bell . . . I recognize its tinkle . . .
Another customer who'll drop

by for Bisto, Bovril, Colman's English Mustard,
liquorice allsorts, lollipops,
War Horse plug tobacco, Gillette razors, Bo-Peeps,
Chivers Jelly, or Bird's Custard.

PIP AND MAGWITCH

In an effort to distract his victim and throw the police off his scent,
Anwar al-Awlaki had left a paperback of *Great Expectations*
all bundled up with a printer-cartridge bomb. They found his
　　fingerprints
on the page—wouldn't you know?—where Dickens,
having put us all in a quandary on the great marshes of Kent,
now sets us down with Pip and the leg-ironed convict, Abel
　　Magwitch,
Pip forever chained to Magwitch by dint
of having brought him a pork pie and file in a little care package.

For the moment, he's a seven-year-old whose Christmas Eve's
　　spent
trying to come up with a way to outfox
this hard-line neighbor, unshaven, the smell of a Polo Mint
not quite masking his breath, his cigar twirling in its unopened
　　sarcophagus
like an Egyptian mummy, one dismissive of the chance
it will ever come into its inheritance.

A DENT

In memory of Michael Allen

The height of one stall at odds with the next in your
    grandfather's byre
where cattle allowed themselves to speak only at Yule
gave but little sense of why you taught us to admire
the capacity of a three-legged stool

to take pretty much everything in its stride,
even the card-carrying Crow who let out a war whoop
now your red pencil was poised above my calf-hide
manuscript like a graip above a groop.

The depth of a dent in the flank of your grandfather's cow
from his having leaned his brow
against it morning and night

for twenty years of milking by hand
gave but little sense of how distant is the land
on which you had us set our sights.

DODGEMS

The pink cloud hanging over Barry's amusement park in Portrush.
So plainspoken, candy floss. The Freemasons' Hall
boarded up for the whole month of August. The almost constant
    rainfall.
We're right between the start of the grouse- and partridge-

shooting seasons. Red sails in the sunset way off Portstewart.
I've resorted to singing "Yellow Polka Dot Bikini"
to the landlady's Pekingese.
The bookcase in the B&B holds Hermann Hesse's *Siddhartha*,

the American first edition. It's 1960. The decade being ushered
in may yet be a decade of selflessness. My hankering for that hula
    hoop
stands in the way of enlightenment. The biplane looping the loop.
Even Ramore Head will have its right shoulder bared

à la Buddha. The wooden roller coaster will eventually get on track.
For now it's all about novelty,
starting with novelty songs. The landlady shyly denies supporting
    Linfield.
Shane Leslie has handed over the deed of Lough Derg

to the Diocese of Clogher. The landlady's demurral
is in strict contrast with these no-nonsense
bumper cars. It cuts no ice with them, the thought of sitting on
    the fence.
I'd hoped a gelato from Morelli's

might help me through the chapter on avarice.
For now I'm joined on the rink by the dodgem boy, an
    out-and-out maniac.
Our electrical pick-up poles are the tails of chipmunks.
Though our celestial canopy is on the fritz,

I'm blessed with a godlike cotton-candy beard.
Our pick-up poles may be quite forthright, our confrontations
    quite unabashed,
but the lambskin apron in which the dodgem boy collects the
    cash
is symbolic of a pure heart.

BARRAGE BALLOONS, BUCK ALEC,
BIRD FLU, AND YOU

for Dermot Seymour

After those first paintings at Art Research and Exchange
I would never again be able to go home, never mind home on
    the range.
The Swede who invented the Aga
had previously lost his sight to an explosion. The rain
    summoned by a blackbird's raga
came sweeping over the Shankill, over the burning car
where Boston and Lowther were dumped, having been fingered
    in the bar
as a Prod and a Pape
enjoying a wee jar together. A wee escapade. A wee escape.

That would have been January 1977, when you were twenty,
    I twenty-five.
An era when we might still devoutly skive
off for the afternoon to the Washington or the Crown Liquor
    Saloon.
Almost every day someone floated a barrage balloon
over the city. We treated the wicker fence
that ran between us with such reverence

it might have been hooked up not to the balloon covered in
    ox-hide strips
but the "ox-hide" ingots of tin from a sunken Phoenician ship.

Until I met you in Tedford's Ship Chandlers, where we'd both
    gone to buy new sails,
I'd assumed the boat I was in was the largest not to use nails.
All along you'd been spirit-gumming a Harrier jump jet
while the wind blew its own trumpet
at the exploits of Buck Alec Robinson and Silver McKee.
In Sailortown alone there were three
of those sweetie shops
where they still sold pieties at a penny a pop.

In the midst of all those sacred cows, in the midst of the fish,
    flesh, and fowl,
we heard only the limer-hounds howl
as they pursued a mountain hare we'd taken as our totem.
Often a swollen scrotum
may not be traced back to an ill-fitting loincloth
just as not all potato diseases may be laid at the door of the potato
    moth.
On Cave Hill, meanwhile, the hunt was on and the time was ripe
for the limer-hounds to revert to type.

Though you may dismiss as utter tosh

my theory this gung-ho stallion's by Bacon out of Bosch,

there's no denying a rooster

will put most of us in a flooster

while the pig that turns out to be less pig than ham

is every bit as alarming. Am I right in thinking that's meant to
be a ram

in a ferraiolo cape?

Hasn't the ewe with scrapie got herself into a scrape?

I don't suppose the moorland streams over which the huntsmen
ride roughshod

and the puddles through which their horses plod

will give rise to enough salmon

to fertilize the soil and stave off another famine.

I hadn't seen the connection between "spade" and "spud"

and "quid" and "cud"

till I noticed the mouth of an Indian elephant from the same
troupe

the filmmakers fitted with "African" ears and tusks was stained
with nettle soup.

It's taken me thirty years to discover the purple dye on your royal
mail

derives not from a sea snail

but the fact you're a scion

of the house in which Buck Alec kept a lion,

albeit a *toothless* lion, which he was given to parade along the

    Old Shore Road.

I still half-expect to meet Buck Alec conducting a merkin-toad

on the end of a piece of Tedford's rope

while decrying as aberrations Henry Joy McCracken and Jemmy

    Hope.

We've all been there, I realize, on the brink

of a butte covered with sea pink

and rising from the swell like an organ pedal.

Think of Kit Carson, Freemason as he was, winning another tin

    medal

for giving the Navajo the old "Get Thee Hence"

from their pinnacle. Although the UK is now under mass

    surveillance

this ram couldn't give a tuppenny tup

about the passing of the cup.

Even Christ's checking us out from his observation post.

Even he can't quite bend *Tiocfaidh Ár Lá* to the tune of "Ghost

Riders in the Sky." An Orangeman in his regalia is still regaling

    us with a sermon

about the ways of Fermanagh men and other vermin.

The Aga-inventor continues to gape

through the streetscape

of smoke and dust and broken glass flickering down like so

    much ticker tape

from the entry into Jerusalem of the King of the Apes.

RITA DUFFY: *WATCHTOWER II*

1

From here it looks as if the whole country is spread under a
    camouflage tarp
rolled out by successive British garrisons
stationed in Crossmaglen. As teenagers we worked our way
    through *Íosagán*
Agus Sgéalta Eile while selling shocks and struts
from a tumbledown garage. Our vision of Four Green Fields
    shrinks to the olive drab
the Brits throw over everything. This must be their version of a
    tour d'horizon,
their scanners scanning our hillsides while we still try to scan
a verse by Pádraig Pearse. One advantage of a farm that, as they
    say, *bestrides*
the border is how industrial diesel
dyed with a green dye ferries itself from the South into the North
by force of gravity alone. The fact that laundered diesel's then
    worth
twice at much at the pump supports the usual
tendencies of the punters to misjudge
our motives and see us as common criminals. Like seeing smoke
    in a paint smudge.

2

One of our neighbors, interned for selling *An Phoblacht*, learned
    we're not the first tribe
to have been put down or the first to have risen
against our oppressors. That's why we've always sided with the
    Redskin
and the Palestinian. It must be because steroids
are legal in the North but not the South the Brits like to eavesdrop
on our comings and goings. As for kerosene,
the fact that it's cheaper in the North is enough to sicken
our happiness. That and the upstarts
who try to horn in on our operation. We're in a constant tussle
with these Seoiníns-come-lately, a constant back-and-forth
on the business of smuggling fuel. We run it through cat litter or
    fuller's earth
to absolve it of the dye. By far the biggest hassle
is trying to get rid of the green sludge
left over from the process. It infiltrates our clothes. It's impossible
    to budge.

A NIGHT ON THE TILES
WITH J. C. MANGAN

1

Some call for "macerated." Some call for "stewed."
The prunes are oddly fizzy
from narcosis.

2

Not that Francis Bacon. *That* Francis Bacon.
The barcode
on the cereal box is Ogham.

3

At least we haven't misconstrued
two eggs over easy
as a lace-frilled pair of knickers.

4

At least we haven't mistaken
a bottle of Paraquat
for a 1990 Château d'Yquem.

5

We'll swear this is the last time as we swore the rain
would never darken our doors again.

SAFFRON

Sometimes I'd happen on Alexander and Cleopatra
and several of their collaborators
tucking into a paella
tinged with saffron, saffron thought to be a cure
for scabies, bloody scours,
fires in the belly,

skin cancer, the ancient pestilence of Sumer,
not to speak of Alzheimer's
and plain old melancholy.
I'm pretty sure things first
started to look bleak in 1987 at the University
of East Anglia

where I was introduced to the art of the lament
by Ezekiel. His electric fire's single element
was an orange ice lolly.
He made me think I might lose my spot
as number one hod carrier in Mesopotamia,
a role that came quite easily

now I lived in a ziggurat
overlooking a man-made lake and sipped sugared

water with a swarm of honeybees.
Though A Flock of Seagulls
were scheduled to play the Union, there had been an icicle
in my heart since Anubis,

half-man, half-jackal,
had palmed me off on Ezekiel
for ritual embalmment.
He claimed A Flock of Seagulls were a one-hit wonder,
desert flowers left high and dry
on the polder. Anubis refused to implement

the Anglo-Irish Agreement.
He also told me the church clock in Crimond
had sixty-one minutes
to the hour. Ezekiel, meanwhile, was convinced
that Creative Writing, still in its infancy,
would amount

to a bona fide
academic pursuit only if students weren't spoon-fed
but came to think of literature
as magical rather than magisterial.
Saffron itself was derived from the three stigma-tufts of a sterile
crocus that, ground, were often adulterated

with turmeric. An icicle was formed
precisely because it would repeatedly warm
to the idea of camaraderie,
then repeatedly give in to chilliness.
I took comfort from the insistence of the anchoress, Julian,
on the utter

necessity of sin for self-knowledge, a theory I'd have to tout
to the Hare Krishna devotees
who'd sworn off sex outside procreation in marriage.
Sometimes I'd see one, late at night, in saffron robe and topknot,
stranded at a bus stop
on the outskirts of Norwich.

AT THE LAB

Somewhere off the Grand Banks
a lapstrake sea that sailed into the teeth
of a gale now foundered on a reef
and promptly sank.

I was at the lab to analyze the spore
in a seaweed wreath
marking the spot where it came to grief,
you the pollen in a sediment core

from a bog in Ireland where, thanks
to its being built plank-upon-plank
(each rig fastened to the one beneath),

a plowed field running alongside the shore
had reached North America before
Eric or Leif.

A CIVIL WAR SUITE

1. MATHEW BRADY:

FIRST BATTLE OF BULL RUN

Wasn't it, after all, Irish riffraff
from the docks of New Orleans,
Irish "wharf rats,"
louts and longshoremen,

Irish toughs and roughs
(any of whom would gleefully drive a lance
through the heart
of William Tecumseh Sherman),

Irish rogues and rapscallions,
culchies and munchies
who'd make up the 1st Louisiana Special Battalion
at the First Battle of Manassas
and allow Brady to become such a dab
hand at fixing that *guerre* in Daguerreotype?

It's hardly too much to trace the "guidon"
to the court of Eleanor of Aquitaine
and her idea of chivalry bred in the bone.
The "loitering" horses about to spill their guts
are by Keats, for sure, but Keats
out of Tennyson.
That "musical clank" is Whitman's alone.

3. LOUIS LANG: *RETURN OF THE 69TH (IRISH) REGIMENT, N.Y.S.M. FROM THE SEAT OF WAR*

It's been just a week since they were seen off
by Stonewall Jackson at Bull Run,
which may be why the only one to doff
his cap as if there might be an outbreak of fun
is Captain Meagher, an intimate of muddling through
since he escaped Van Diemen's Land in 1852.
You'll notice how a smoothbore gun

of the type Meagher favors for close combat
has found its way into the hands
of two brothers who are themselves in a spat
as to why a bayonet might expand
on an entry wound. Sometimes it's only by a crowded pier
we recognize what we hold dear.
The rifle points toward the linen bands

in which Sergeant Tracy's own wounds are wrapped.
His wife helps him off the baggage cart.
Lieutenant Nugent's right arm is strapped

awkwardly in a sling. The crowd must surely part
before these six or seven drummer boys.
We can all but hear the poise
they bring to those snare drums. It's a tribute to Lang's art

that we might for a moment forget the sniper
to whom so much of this may be assigned
and focus on an uilleann piper
lodged in the shadows, for when it comes to what lies behind
the impulse to fade
into the background at this or any parade
the truth is he's no less blind

to us than we are to him.
I doubt somehow he'll ever make a start
on learning "The Battle Hymn
of the Republic." I suppose some might take heart
from Father O'Reilly confiding in a widow how this cup
will pass while drawing up
a slightly revised version of the heaven chart

or the half-smile on a man who greets his child
for the first time, or the non-sniper up a tree,
or even the piper who's beguiled
Meagher into thinking Ireland might soon be free.

Stooped though he may be over his chanter and drones,
he raises everything a semitone
and allows us for the first time to see

beyond the harbor sky with its rents and rips
to what is now a no-fly dome
where we at last begin to get to grips
with the discontinued Kodachrome
of our great transports
that hardly ever put into ports
and our flag-draped coffins secretly airlifted home.

.

4. EMILY DICKINSON: "A SLASH OF BLUE—A SWEEP OF GRAY"

Here some still scout
a vineyard path
to trample out
the grapes of wrath . . .
How many died
in the bloodbath?
This side? That side?
You do the math.

5. SALLY MANN: *MANASSAS*

Less the idea of what the world might be "like"
than what it is "like *photographed*"
has had us lug
over glacier-grooved

and -polished mountains what we once took
for luggage, bags of hominy grits,
barrels of pork and hardtack,
wall-to-wall crates

of wet-glass negatives,
the tackle by which we still hold on with grim
determination to our salt codfish,
the portable darkroom
in which we've yet to cure
ourselves of the idea that art is "pure" or "impure."

RECALCULATING

1

Arthritis is to psoriasis as Portugal is to Brazil.
Brazil is to wood as war club is to war.
War is to wealth as performance is to appraisal.
Appraisal is to destiny as urn is to ear.

Ear is to grasshopper as China is to DDT.
Tea is to leaf as journalist is to source.
Source is to leak as Ireland is to debt.
Debt is to honor as arthritis is to psoriasis.

2

Wait. Isn't arthritis to psoriasis as Brazil is to Portugal?
Portugal is to fado as Boaz is to Ruth.
Ruth is to cornfield as wave is to particle.

3

Particle is to beach as pebble is to real estate.

Realty is to reality as sky is to earth.

Earth is to all ye know as done is to dusted.

WE LOVE THE HORSE
BECAUSE ITS HAUNCH

We love the horse because its haunch
most brings to mind our own,
its back to a wall of freezing rain
that's mounting a smear campaign.
An ancient riverbed on Mars
throws up the rounded stones
prized less by quarriers
or men given to hoist the hod
than those who hope still to relaunch
a phalanx (cf. *planche*)
of Roman catapults
from a refitted aircraft carrier.
Once Roman women went so far
as to set up a cult

to rival that of great mother
Cybele, Cybele
the goddess of bee dunes and buzz drones
lodging in the frontal bone,
whose braids have always been unclasped,

her hair *tri na cheile*
like the mare's before a farrier
who is himself somewhat slipshod.
Little has looked more through-other
than the old lime pother
where two smiths go at it
hammer and tongs, two border terriers
with their many hoof-knives and rasps
scattered in the horse shit

while they try to wrangle the hoop
off a chariot wheel.
Until now, that is, when Cybele
opens fire on the bailey
where the Normans have learned to cant
the rim of that same wheel.
A young marsh-harrier
will go traipsing through air it's trod
because it's out of the loop,
only gradually learning to stoop
as a fully fledged hawk
attempting to break the sound barrier.
Those whose experience is scant
will most enjoy the chalk

downs and all such pleasant vistas

afforded by tunics,

by plackets or stomachers that seal

almost more than they reveal

when ripped open, by Jove . . .

As to which war, it was the Second Punic

where a spear carrier

who'd himself been given a prod

because he'd somehow just missed a

cue claimed four ballistas

set off the string quartet

in the spirit of "the more the merrier."

It was those catapults that drove

Roman women to let

their hair grow right down to their waists

for twisting into skeins

and stretching our sense of the funic-

ular to modern Munich.

Some early fragmentation bombs

were the calcified brains

of Celtic warriors

(i.e., Mesgegra, Oh my God!),

against which combatants have faced

off and straightaway braced
themselves with the staunchness
of such practiced feinters and parriers
as two girls at a senior prom
who've worn the same slit dress.

ANONYMOUS: FROM "MARBAN AND GUAIRE"

KING GUAIRE

My brother Marban, hermit monk,
why don't you sleep in a bed
instead of among pine trees, with only the forest floor
on which to lay your tonsured head?

MARBAN THE HERMIT

As it happens, I have a hut in the forest.
Its precise location
is known only to God, but I can report
that on one side an ash tree stands guard
while the other is barred
by a hazel such as you'd find at a ringfort.

Heather stands in for its doorposts
and fragrant honeysuckle
binds its lintel fast.
For the benefit of the pigs
beech trees let fall beech twigs
and pig-fattening mast.

The dimensions of my hut—
small but not *too* small—
make it easy enough to defend.
A woman in the guise of a blackbird
spreads the word
from its gable end.

The great stags of Drum Rolach
start up from a stream that runs
across a mud shelf.
From there you may make out
clay-red Roigne, Mucruime and, no doubt,
the plain of Moenmag itself.

Won't you come for a tour
of my wooded realm
with its paths only wild beasts beat?
Though I know
you have much more to show,
my life is quite replete.

Think of the shaggy limbs
of a yew tree
saying its sooth.

Think of a massive oak
spreading a green cloak
by way of a summer booth.

You may ponder a huge apple tree such
as you'd find at another ringfort.
A tree bestowing many gifts.
When it comes to nuts,
the hazel trees by my hut
never give short shrift.

There are the best of wells
and lovely waterfalls
over which to gush.
The medicinal yew
and hackberry on which to chew
are nowhere more lush.

In the vicinity are goats,
stags, and hinds,
pigs that are the next best thing to pets,
and wild pigs lurking in the scrub,
the badger sow and her cubs
in their sett.

In front of my establishment
a great host of the countryside peaceably assembles.
They gather. They gather and fold.
Meanwhile the dog-fox
picking its way through the wood in long socks
is lovely to behold.

In the face of the quickly prepared repasts
on offer in my house
I couldn't be more devout.
The water's superb,
as are the perennial herbs
that accompany salmon and trout.

The rowan or mountain ash.
The blackthorn and the sloes
within its scope.
Acorns in an acorn heap.
A bunch of bare berry-sheep
dangling from bare mountain slopes.

A handful of eggs,
honey, more beech mast, heath pease
God's sent my way.

There are even more apples to prog,
cranberries from the bog,
and berries known as whortle-, bil-, or blae-.

Beer flavored with bog myrtle.
A bed of strawberries the only bed
from which joy is evinced.
Hawthorn good for a pain in the heart.
Yew for giving it a start.
Blackthorn tea for a medicinal rinse.

How lovely then to quaff a cup
of hazel mead
from the very freshest batch.
To nibble at more acorns
and blackberries among the flailing thorns
of the bramble patch.

In next to no time summer has come round
with its dense ground cover
and all it bespeaks.
The tastes of wild marjoram
and, near the pond dam,
blood-cleansing wild leeks.

Bright-breasted wood pigeons
will be billing and cooing
in a lovely rush.
Over my abode
the default mode
of a mistle thrush.

Bees and beetles,
their low-level hum
as if through a screen.
Brent geese and barnacle geese
disturbing the peace
just before Halloween.

A lithe little linnet
working his magic
from the hazel branch.
It's on an open door the flock
of variegated woodpeckers knock.
They give themselves carte blanche.

Now white seabirds come flying,
herons and gulls
and the sea airs they bruit.

Far from down in the dumps
is the grouse's thump
through red heather shoots.

Then the heifer lowing
in high summer,
daylight on the gain.
Life is far from tough
when we've more than enough
from the bounteous plain.

The call of the wind
through a wood's wickerwork.
Clouds that somehow prevail.
A river that falls
through rocky walls
on such a pleasant scale.

Beautiful, too, the pine trees
that give me music
without my making a pitch.
However wealthy you may be
Christ has left me
no less rich.

Though you delight
in having more treasures
than might easily have sufficed,
I'm quite content
with what is lent
me by that self-same Christ.

I have none of the aggravation
or din of battle
by which your heartstrings are constantly cut,
only gratitude to the Lord
for the gifts he affords
me in my hut.

KING GUAIRE

I would give my kingdom
and all that's due
to me from Colmán for the rest of my days
to live, Marban, as you.

FEDERICO GARCÍA LORCA: "DEATH"

What a tremendous effort they all put into it!
The horse does its damnedest
to become a dog.
The dog tries so hard to become a swallow.
The swallow busies itself with becoming a bee.
The bee does its level best to become a horse.
As for the horse,
just look at the barbed arrow it draws from the rose,
that faint rose lifting from its underlip.
The rose, meanwhile,
what a slew of lights and calls
are bound up in the living sugar of its stem.
The sugar, in turn,
those daggers it conjures while standing watch.
The little daggers themselves,
such a moon minus horse stalls, such nakedness,
such robust and ruddy skin as they're bent upon.
And I, perched on the gable end,
what a blazing angel I aim at being, and am.
The arch made of plaster, however—
how huge, how invisible, then how small it is,
without the least striving.

A PILLAR

Of the two on an Elizabethan stage
meant to support the heavens, one's been itemized
as missing since the flit from Shoreditch
left it high and dry
and safe from our cutthroat Doge.
Once it propped up the drunken sailor on a mast

ready with every nod to tumble down,
once obscured a lady in a doublet
yet to be revealed as the long-lost twin
of Starveling or Snug or Sly.
Many an imp from the Forest of Arden
who scaled it with a catapult

or pail of birdlime made from holly bark
to trap a mistle thrush or canary
has returned a confirmed empiric,
extending the use of birdlime to the nether eye
and the bugle hung in an invisible baldric
as a cure for gonorrhea

while poling still across the Thames-Isis.
There we played ducks and drakes

with our cutthroat Dogberry and all those so-and-sos
determined to try
us at the next assizes.
Our conversation about the intrigue

in which the lad dressed as a lady dressed as a lad
who proved the ferret
to your own coney burrow and took such delight
in being singled out as a double-dealing spy
by both Old Gobbo and Lancelot
must have been overheard

by Snug in the shadow of this very pillar . . .
Its shadow lengthened even as
the sun struggled to raise a beam from the blur
and we fell in with the hue and cry
of men-at-arms on the trail of the old King's player
who stole from house to house

in an effort to put himself beyond the reach
of tub-fast and mercuric sulfide.
Now we take comfort in this one-legged arch
beyond which the sky
is leveling a charge
of which we may never be absolved.

CATAMARAN

Between Dominica and Martinique
we go in search of sperm whales, listening for their
    tink-tink-tink
on a hydrophone
hooked up to a minispeaker. A prisoner's tap
on a heating pipe . . .
The one faint hope by which he's driven.

My son is reading *Lord of the Flies*. I can think of that book
only as the dog-eared manuscript Charles Monteith would pick
out of the slush pile at Faber's.
I'm pretty sure dear Charles recognized
a version of himself in Piggy. The same prep-school anguish.
Same avuncularity. Same avoirdupois.

Now I imagine lying by my dead wife
just as a sperm whale lies by its dead mate as if
it might truly be said to mourn.
A corruption of the Tamil term for "two logs
lashed together with rope or the like,"
the word we use is "catamaran."

NEAR THE GRACE OF GOD NAIL SALON

In the slave castle at Cape Coast
I saw slaves pushed from pillar to whipping post
on their way out of Ghana
by the Door of No Return.
I suppose any plain-backed pipit might learn
to sound the vox humana

from its organ reed, given how a woman may take wing
above an open sewer and sing,
making not only her own spirits quicken
but gladdening the heart of a boy who trots in her wake.
She glances back to where the boy (her son?) makes
like that mangy chicken

shooting its cuffs because its suit's so hot.
It being noon, she hasn't much of a shot
at casting a shadow,
even though she carries home
a mess of fish in a basket set on a blue latex foam
mattress pad no

self-respecting fish would be seen dead on.
Near the Grace of God Nail Salon

she pauses to take the basket
from her head,
as though to ponder if she might choose, instead
of a fish-shaped casket,

a casket in the shape of a beer bottle or speedboat.
The mangy chicken, plus a mangy goat,
chime in with the plain-backed pipit
to celebrate her setting the basket back atop
her head as she draws level with the Vote for Jesus Wig Shop.
If there's a balance now I'm inclined to tip it

in favor of the boy who comes back double quick
to seize my wrist despite its being slick
with suntan lotion.
After his recent brush with mange
he, too, is able to rearrange
himself with almost as little commotion—

with almost as little to-do—
as the military coup
that ousted Kwame Nkrumah.
Now I see that his entire outfit, from his football shirt
to his sneakers shining in the dirt,
comes courtesy of Puma.

A GIRAFFE

Though her lorgnette
and evening gloves
suggest she's made for the role
of an opera buff
singing along with the score,
her mouth's out of sync
with her own overdub.

A giraffe that flubbed
her lines coming back to drink
just a little more
of the bubbly stuff
from the dried-out mud hole
in which a reflection of
her upper body's already set.

DROMEDARIES AND DUNG BEETLES

An eye-level fleck of straw in the mud wall
is almost as good as gold . . .
I've ventured into this piss-poor urinal
partly to escape the wail
of thirty milch camels with their colts

as they're readied for our trek
across the dunes, partly because I've guzzled
three glasses of the diuretic
gunpowder tea the Tuareg
hold in such esteem. Their mostly business casual

attire accented by a flamboyant
blue or red nylon grab rope
round their lower jaws, dromedaries point
to a 9-to-5 life of knees bent
in the service of fetching carboys

and carpetbags from A to B across the scarps.
Think Boyne coracles
bucking from wave to wave. Think scarab
beetles rolling their scrips
of dung to a gabfest. These dromedary-gargoyles

are at once menacing and meek
as, railing against their drivers' kicks and clicks,
they fix their beautiful-ugly mugs
on their own Meccas.
The desert sky was so clear last night the galaxies

could be seen to pulse . . .
The dromedaries were having a right old chin-wag,
each musing on its bolus.
Every so often one would dispense some pills
that turned out to be generic

sheep or goat. The dung beetles set great store
not by the bitter cud
nor the often implausible *Histories*
of Herodotus but the stars
they use to guide

themselves over the same sand dunes
as these thirty milch camels
and their colts. They, too, make a continuous
line through Algeria and Tunisia.
Dung beetles have been known to positively gambol

on the outskirts of Zagora, a boom-
town where water finds it hard not to gush

over the date palms.
Despite the clouds of pumice
above Marrakesh even I might find my way to Kesh,

in the ancient barony of Lurg,
thanks to Cassiopeia
and her self-regard. Think of how there lurks
in almost all of us a weakness for the allegorical.
Think of a Moroccan swallow's last gasp

near the wattle-and-daub oppidum
where one of my kinsmen clips
the manes of a groaning chariot team . . .
Think of Private Henry Muldoon putting his stamp
on the mud of Gallipoli

on August 8, 1915. It appears
he worked as a miner at Higham Colliery
before serving in the Lancasters and the 8th Welsh Pioneers.
His somewhat pronounced ears
confirm his place in the family gallery.

"It's only a blink . . ." my father used to say. "Only a blink."
I myself seem to have developed the gumption
to stride manfully out of a neo-Napoleonic
latrine and play my part in the march on Casablanca
during the North African campaign.

SOME PITFALLS AND HOW TO AVOID THEM

for Asher

Stratocumulus, or cumulonimbus, the clouds have made such
    strides
in crossing the Rockies
they've now caught up with us. A diet of buffalo ragout
will leave anyone "in straits"

sooner rather than later. That the glister in a Port-a-John
on a parking lot near Bennigan's
in Fargo, North Dakota, turned out to be a pine cone
doesn't mean the Cheyenne

were wrong to take things at face value.
Bear in mind that "calomel" looks a lot like "chamomile"
to the guy trying to compile
a camping checklist. Given the near certainty they'll fall foul

of some infection of the blood,
snakebite, sundry blisters and boils,
syphilis, dysentery, piles,
and plain old costiveness, Lewis and Clark plied

their entire squad

with Dr. Rush's Bilious Pills,

the upshot being the Corps of Discovery would loosen their
    bowels

by thunderclaps and quicksilver-scoots

through random pine scrub and clumps of river birch.

Now we've pulled into the Samurai

Sushi Bar and ordered two Godzilla rolls. Bear in mind that Zimri

was king of Israel only as long as it took to purge

himself of himself. Who would have guessed

that J.M.W. Turner was perfecting his ability to scumble

cumulonimbus and stratocumulus

precisely as Lewis and Clark reached the Pacific coast

and built Fort Clatsop? The Cheyenne chewed the gum

of both ponderosa

and lodgepole pines. Bear in mind how our fireside banter

may be lost to the generations to come

but their native scouts

will still be able to follow our route across America

by the traces of mercury

in our scats.

CUBA (2)

I'm hanging with my daughter in downtown Havana.
She's worried people think she's my mail-order bride.
It might be the *Anseo* tattooed on her ankle.
It might be the tie-in with that poem of mine.

The '59 Buicks. The '59 Chevys.
The '59 Studebakers with their whitewalled wheels.
The rain-bleached streets have been put through a mangle.
The sugar mills, too, are feeling the squeeze.

We touch on how Ireland will be inundated
long before the nil-nil draw.
Che Guevara's father was one of the Galway Lynches.
Now a genetically engineered catfish can crawl

on its belly like an old-school guerrilla.
Maybe a diminished seventh isn't the note
a half-decent revolution should end on?
The poor with their hands out for "pencils" and "soap"?

Hopped up though I am on caffeine
I've suffered all my life from post-traumatic fatigue.

Even a world-class sleeper like Rip Van Winkle
was out of it for only twenty years.

A fillet of the fenny
cobra may yet fold into a blood-pressure drug.
A passion for marijuana
may yet be nipped in the bud.

Some are here for a nose job. Some a torn meniscus.
The profits from health tourism have been salted away.
The blue scorpion takes the sting from one cancer.
Ovarian may yet leave us unfazed.

Hemingway's sun hat is woven from raffia.
He's tried everything to stop the rot.
He's cut everything back to the bare essentials.
His '55 Chrysler's in the shop.

We'll sit with Hemingway through yet another evening
of trying to stay off the rum.
I'm running down the list of my uncles.
It was Uncle Pat who was marked by a gun.

Our friends Meyer Lansky and the Jewish mafia
built the Riviera as a gambling club.

Had it not been for the time differential
Uncle Arnie might have taken a cut.

The best baseball bats are turned from hibiscus.
They're good against people who get in your way.
The best poems, meanwhile, give the answers
to questions only they have raised.

We touch on Bulat and Yevgeny,
two Russian friends who've since left town.
The Cuban ground iguana
is actually quite thin on the ground.

The cigars we lit up on Presidents' Avenue
have won gold medals in the cigar games.
Now it seems a cigar may twinkle
all the more as the light fails.

My daughter's led me through Hemingway's villa
to a desk round which dusk-drinkers crowd.
She insists the *Anseo* on her Achilles tendon
represents her being in the here and now.

The cattle egret is especially elated
that a plow may still be yoked to an ox.

Others sigh for the era of three-martini lunches
and the Martini-Henry single-shot.

When will we give Rothstein and Lansky and their heavies
the collective heave?
In Ireland we need to start now to untangle
the rhetoric of 2016.

The Riviera's pool is shaped like a coffin.
So much has been submerged here since the Bay of Pigs.
Maybe that's why the buildings are wrinkled?
Maybe that's why the cars have fins?

TUSKER

Given that she does nothing by halves
it was hard to see how the wunderkind surgeon from the burn
    unit would salve
her conscience while trying to keep cool

in the face of a barstool
covered in a whale's foreskin. A yacht on which the swimming pool
converts to a dance floor? It was Aristotle Onassis

who rescued that concept, just as he reclaimed the word "nauseous"
for the shipping industry. The rings in their noses
will prevent overindulgence in beech mast

in a high percentage of hogs but to help them stand fast
against worms a garlic-and-molasses supplement is unsurpassed.
I was feeling such bonhomie

this morning partly because of the burn unit phenom's
evident compassion for the bonham
she was about to sweal

over a Bunsen burner in anticipation of what this might reveal
about the capacity of singed skin to heal.
Last night Hippocrates had prescribed pig fat and vinegar

wrapped around the middle finger
to another freethinker
who'd abandoned (or been abandoned by?) the god

who once clawed
his way out from under six feet of his native sod.
It's inevitable that at least some of the cream and treacle

fed to a tusker will trickle
from his jaws like blood from Dracula.
I was feeling so expansive today at the pig mart

also because I'd met another Large White boar with just one
    moving part
and vowed to donate to him, if not my heart,
then at least a heart valve.

HONEY

Our plane takes hill upon hill long since cleared of pines. The flash
of matching lakelets. Weather and more weather.
The copilot points to at least one benefit
of felling pines for warship keels, namely how the heather
that pits itself against an old saw pit
and fills in the great gash
of a logging road also sustains our friends the honeybees.

The coroner at the scene of the crash
found the seams of Buddy Holly's jacket of yellow faux leather
"split almost full-length" and his skull also "split."
Buddy's personal effects amounted to a pair of cufflinks together
with the top of a ballpoint pen and, barely within his remit,
the $193.00 in cash
from which the coroner deducted $11.65 in fees.

SEVEN SELFIES FROM THE CHÂTEAU D'IF

1

I too was flung into a cell so dark
I'd hunger for the black and moldy bread
that all too soon defined my comfort zone.
I cast my mind back for some ill-judged phrase,
unguarded look, circumstance I'd misread,
some vibe I gave at which some took offense.

2

I too have heard another scratch his mark
with such conviction as might match my own.

3

I too was schooled by a high-minded monk
who ruled the world-book must be read aloud.

4

It took both winter freeze and summer freeze
to yield growth rings so uniformly dense
my tone brought back a Stradivarius—
demure-insistent, delicate-immense.

5

I too switched with a dead man in his bunk
and stitched myself into his burlap shroud.

6

I too have heard ghoulish pallbearers scoff
while I've kept cool and clutched my toothbrush shank.

7

I too am hurtling down with such great force
it's even harder to keep playing dead

while knowing in my bones I shouldn't tense
myself for impact. Soon I will slit the cloth
and, having freed one arm, then free my head
and hope to surface far from where I sank.

THE FIRING SQUAD

*I am going to tell you something I never but once let out of the bag before
and that was just after I reached London and before I had begun to value
myself for what I was worth. It is a very damaging secret and you may
not thank me for taking you into it when I tell you that I have often
wished I could be sure that the other sharer of it had perished in the war.
It is this: The poet in me died nearly ten years ago.* —ROBERT FROST
TO LOUIS UNTERMEYER, MAY 4, 1916

*I am very happy I am dying for the glory of God and the honour
of Ireland.* —JOSEPH MARY PLUNKETT TO FATHER
SEBASTIAN, MAY 4, 1916

Something I never but once let on
is that I am as ready to be hanged, drawn,
and quartered as the Blessed Oliver, as ready as his sober-suited
descendant, Joseph Mary Plunkett,
to be shot—all the more so if I've married my beloved Grace
only hours before. Like many of my race,
I've come to see English plantain as a flatfooted
weed terminating in an oblongoid

spike of flowers like the head of a mace.
It tends to establish itself in the least likely place,
exercising a feudal

droit du seigneur on pavements, parking lots where battery
acid and diesel have bled
into the soil, drive-ins where we're wooed by, and wed
to, the whole kit and caboodle
of empire. As for a priest or padre

laying about him with his holy-water sprinkler, it has me see red
no less than if he wielded a flint ax-head
made by an old-style flint knapper.
That's why I get up from my pillow (filled, as it happens, with
    buckwheat)
to set my face against the dawn.
As I stride out now across the Institute lawn
I look all the more dapper
for the white handkerchief so firmly lodged in my breast pocket.

ÁLVARO DE CAMPOS: "BELFAST, 1922"

While a great gantry
at the head of the lough
continues to stand sentry
a team of shipyard men rush to caulk

a seam. No dunnock in a choir
of dunnocks will relent
from claiming as its own the gore
of land on which Harland

and Wolff is built. Catching a rivet
in a pair of tongs
and banging it into a rift
will hardly mend it. The dun in *dun*nock

doesn't allow for the dash
of silver in its head and throat feathers.
Because chicks within one clutch
often have different fathers,

dunnocks are at once highly territorial
and likely to go unremarked.
Though they've been known to drill
in Glenavy and Deer Park,

the dunchered shipyard men are no less peaceable
than those of Barrow-in-Furness.
Souped up, staid, swerveless, supple,
they hold in equal reverence

the pennywhistle and the plenilunar
pigskin of a Lambeg drum,
be they sending off a White Star liner
or a little tramp.

LOS DISSIDENTES

Coming to anything late in the day has an allure
all its own. The river plummets here with such aplomb
it brings back Slim Pickens's holler
as he bronco-busts the H-bomb

in *Dr. Strangelove*. We like it when things are stacked
against us, when beavers are showing
initiative at the beaver dam. We take comfort from the fact
that after years of scenery-chewing

Rockets Redglare thoroughly upped
his profile with his role in *Down by Law*.
Though the file

is almost certainly corrupt,
we can still hope to salvage something from the raw
footage of the waterfall.

REQUIRED FIELDS

Then we could ride all day and yet
not reach the farthest edge of our demesne,
its slow handclap of grouse
impatient for the mist-wreathed
curtain of the moor
to rise. Remember the beech
where we were filed
under our noms de plume,
the chestnut tree where a soul was known to roost

before it was set in linotype
or its path laid
in herringbone? For a second asterisk
we'd use a dagger, then double daggers
for the third footnote.
There was a time when accountants took into account
our dim view of paying tax.
Now so much else dims
while the phonograph bends its ear

toward the ice trumpet. Yes. The ice trumpet
recorded in the Ice Hotel

that we now favor over Strauss.
An impasto sheep
well used to some rule of thumb
poses with a donkey-easel
against a hemmed-in sky.
Along the fraying torrent
that itself runs along the stage

the deerhounds strut and fret.
Then we had something like free rein
to laugh with the half-crazed maid from *Die Fledermaus*
who laughed till her bosom heaved
uncontrollably. The horse manure
smelling of bleach,
how artfully *that* was piled!
I think of the stable groom
turned tour guide who's still known to boost

his minimum wage
by dressing up as a bit of a swell.
They found a credit-card receipt for petrol used to douse
the barn and set fire to a Jeep.
The stable walls were *opus spicatum*.
Everybody knows that teazle
is the prototype of the hook and eye.

It was that stable groom, I'll warrant,
who made a strumpet

of not only Colonel Knipe's
but our own kitchen maid—
the one with the "slipped disc."
My gelding once again took the head staggers
just as I was taking a straw vote
as to whether I should mount
a campaign. Someone brought an ax
to bear on why we'd carved our pseudonyms
on a tree. Was it for fear

we might someday be reconciled
to the idea we can maintain
this tumbledown old manor house
only because we've bequeathed
it to the nation? As it is, guided tour after guided tour
brings home to each
of us how we've let
go of all but seven rooms
to which, we overhear, we are "reduced."

TO MARKET, TO MARKET

I

I'm sure one of the reasons J. J. Astor had been under such
    duress
was that he recently leaned over to the lady seated next to him at
    a dinner party
and wiped his hands on her muslin dress . . .

Maybe he'd had a little too much of a Bordeaux
run up by Phelan or Lynch,
two Irish chemists vying for parity

with Boyle and Beaufort. Treacle bread and cheese in
    cheesecloth, that's the lunch
my father carries as he stands in line
in this predawn dark, waiting for a mower-laden truck to launch

him beyond the realm of the Guatemalans
with whom he tries to keep abreast. Their Igloo coolers are
    packed with beans and rice
in anticipation of their being hired for the day by Princeton
    Complete Lawn.

2

After a day of shouldering bales of cauliflowers in the pouring
  rain
my back was itself a broad leaf, rainwater coursing down the
  groove of its mid-vein.

NOAH & SONS

1

A solitary ewe stood guard
like a widow in her mantle
at the entrance to the graveyard.
One line ran all the way from my pommel through my cantle

to the Massey Ferguson baler
while lovers screamed with tumult harsh
and a converted whaler
sank slowly into the alder marsh.

As we cantered across the stubble
we managed to double
back on ourselves like hares
fleeing a primal scene
to which we're bound to repair
as long as yellow + blue = green.

2

For "ewe" read "yew."
For "baler" read "thrasher."
For "retina" read "retinue."
For "Ashur" read "Asher."

For "fathead" read "minnow."
For "shame" read "Shem."
For "window" read "winnow."
For "bract" read "stem."

For "missile" read "Missal."
For "darnel" read "thistle."
For "skewered" read "skewed."
For "hart" read "chart."
For "Freud" read "feud."
For "dirt" read "dart."

3

Now we were galloping across the swamp
showing little or no decorum,
little or no pomp.
This wasn't the first time we'd had three or four
jorums

too many. For years the heavens had pummeled
us not only with regulation hail
but blow bolts fledged with the comal
tufts of bulrush or cattail.

It seemed marsh elder still made for a blowgun
that raised itself like its own slogan
while "Bring it on"
was the rallying cry
of the thistles now at daggers drawn
that had once seen eye to eye.

PAUL MULDOON: "POMPEII"

1

On the street a boy still mends
a puncture on his bike,

paying out an inner tube
from a tire

and keeping an eye out for a ripple
in the plastic basin.

Like trying to cajole
a red-bellied snake

from the hood of an Oldsmobile
on which it basks.

Jayne's rubberized bathing costume.
How that costume clung.

2

It was during the Festival of the Kalends
we'd seen something of a spike

in the ratings when an ice cube
had all but set fire

to Jayne's right nipple.
A pneumatic caisson

was used less for digging coal
than tunnels. Part of my mistake

was that roses and steel
may both be termed "damask."

Then there's the rose that blooms
on a coal miner's lung.

3

A bridge builder will get the bends
if his coworkers hike

him too suddenly. Her trip to Jiffy Lube
had Jayne aspire

to a McDonald's Triple.
A sex game involving asphyxiation

conjured by bubbles from a pinprick hole.
The surface those bubbles break

likely to reveal
itself only in the sense a mask

reveals who's lain with whom.
The tire's black dog. The inner tube's dog tongue.

CAMILLE PISSARRO: *APPLE PICKING AT ERAGNY-SUR-EPTE*

Christ may as well have been hanged
for a sheep as a lamb,
given how the so-called panking pole
loosening a dam
of apples lodged between boles
is used by one of the work gang

to pierce his side. His garment
strewn on the grass
is a shadow without a seam.
Two of the women grub in the morass
for anything they might deem
salvageable after attacks by varmints

of various stripes. A third stares at his rib cage,
stifling her gasp
in anticipation of another gush of blood
and water. The centurion grasps
his pole more tightly as if the flash flood
of apples might be about to gauge

its own significance.
That middle-distant horse asleep between the shafts
is at least absolved of the mounting block.
Given the successive grafts
of noble scions upon noble stocks,
when I glance

from my hotel window
even I discern
a possibility
I might too readily have spurned—
that any of these rangy, raw-boned trees
is the one I will turn into.

DIRTY DATA

The bog is fenced up there on Slieve Gullion, Slieve Gullion
    where the bracken leaf
 still lies behind the Celto-Iberian sword design
 adopted by the Romans. Pontius Pilate's poised with his
    handkerchief
at the parting spine

where the contestants snort and stamp.
That's right, Lew, the dealing
men from Crossmaglen put whiskey in our piñon tea. A
    hurricane lamp
shines from a shieling

like an undercover star. The goshawk nests in lodgepole and
    ponderosa pine
while a Mescalero girl twists
osiers into a basket that does indeed imitate

what passes for life, given how ring wants nothing more than to
    intertwine
with ring. The mountain's covered in heavy schists.
The streams themselves are muddied.

The dog is tense. The dog is tense the day Ben Hourihane
falls fuel of the new Roman turbine,
Little Miss Sally hisself, tense enough to set off a chain
of events that will see Ben mine

warehouse after warehouse of schlock
and link him via a Roman warship
to a hell-for-leather chariot race at Antioch.
Sooner or later Messala will need a lot more than a double hip

replacement while Ben will barely chafe
at the bit. That's right, Messala, an *amputation* saw!
The doctor is cocking an ear to your chest's tumble-de-drum

like a man trying to open a safe.
To add to the confusion, Ben's still trying to crack a lobster claw
with a lobster claw made of titanium.

Ben has somehow been playing scuffle on his washboard abs
while eating all that treif.
It looks like 1961. Or '65. No time before a few squatters from
    the prefabs
in Dungannon morph into the crowd the paratroopers strafe

on Bloody Sunday. A golden dolphin marks the lap run by each
    new
Roman tribune. Whitelaw. Pym. Rees. Mason.
Atkins. Prior. Hurd. King. Brooke. Mayhew.
Dense, too, the fog when each Halloween Ben ducks in an
    enamel basin

for an enamel apple
and comes up with a botched job.
Such is the integrity of their kraal the horses will find no slot

in the funeral cortege of Winston Churchill from the Royal
    Chapel
to Woodstock. As his carriage passes the dolphins bob
for a commoner's mere 19- rather than a no-stops-pulled 21-gun
    salute.

Along the Thames, meanwhile, even the cranes will bow
and scrape as the coffin passes the Isle of Dogs and the citizenry
    grapple
with their sense of loss. The *Havengore*'s prow
will no more shake off a water dapple

than we'll concede we've been excluded from a race.
It looks as if Little Miss Messala, played by a Belfast boy, will
    clutch
at the idea he might drive a tea-chest bass
to victory. Ben paces the afterdeck in the knowledge that as much

as we have sheltered them
our children will now feel obliged to shelter us
from some harshness we're not fit to bear. They'll glom onto the
    gliomach

shut out of its *lorica segmentata* while expecting us to condemn
wholesale the tattooed gulpin, the tatty glamour-puss,
not to speak of the other stuff they know we'll find hard to
    stomach.

That's right, Lew, you'll have Ben pace the afterdeck of a war galley
to which he's been consigned for having made an ad hominem
remark about a minister who banned a civil rights rally.
Though the top hem

of my childhood bedroom curtain's concealed by a pelmet
it clearly has the makings of a Roman cape.
Take the idea of a bird nesting in a bicycle helmet
some kid's hung by the garage door. The nest follows the nape

no less intently than the truth twisters and tub thumpers
will relocate your *Ben Hur: A Tale of the Christ*
from Judaea to an army outpost

near Jonesborough or Cullaville. These wouldn't be the first
    parachute jumpers
to have been enticed
into a honeypot and then by honeybees beset.

Sometimes the elephant in the room's the single war elephant
Caesar loosed on the Britons one bank-holiday weekend the
    traffic was bumper-
to-bumper. To add to the confusion, the evidence is scant
that the Hourihanes were ever actually reduced to eating Lumpers

in the 1830s. They may well have lived in the nether regions
of Tyrone where the Famine wouldn't hit so hard. That's right,
    Lew, they weren't swept
underfoot by the Ninth Legion
along with the rest of the evidence. Why did someone try to
    intercept

your letter to Billy the Kid? In 1933, Seosamh Mac Grianna would
    follow word for word
your purple-inked prose
as he rendered *Ben Hur* into Gaelic for An Gúm.

To add to the confusion the bird
has single-mindedly begun to transpose
materials from an abandoned site—cloak wool, horsehair, an
    eagle plume.

That's right, Lew, what we're looking at is a feather from a hawk
    or bald eagle
worn by the girl to whom you yourself transferred
your affections shortly after you were appointed to that regal (or
    viceregal)
post in New Mexico. Many of us remember how you'd gird

your loins for a three-day fact-finding mission
with Willie Whitelaw. That's when we first saw Messala twitch
through the partition
in a cowshed where he'd been tortured as a snitch

by four Mescaleros. Messala wouldn't have been the first soldier
    to marry
a local girl. Nor would he have been the first to spill
his guts under interrogation. Did Christ offer Ben water from
    an 1858 army canteen

or the 1874 model? It was on the rifle range at Barry's
amusement park that Ben may first have thought of countering
    the shoot-to-kill
policy by which Billy the Kid was gunned down.

Ben knows a Barrett semiautomatic rifle fitted with a Vari-X sight
    has got the job done
at distances of over a mile. There's really no way to parry
that infrared light. As to who masterminded the bomb run,
the records are almost as fragmentary

as the tile that clattered down from the roof of Ben's council flat
and spooked the prefect's mount.
The Lincoln County War, in which you tried to intervene, was
    another tit-for-tat
war fought between Prods and Papes. The body count

should include the glamour-puss Haya Harareet
as Esther. It must have been during the process of data capture
there was some mash-up of the "coyote brush"

and her little "pleat."
Then there's Cathy O'Donnell, who plays Tirzah, "she who brings
    rapture,"
and on whom Messala might once have had a crush.

The shieling on Slieve Gullion. Oíche Shamhna. Messala's head
     shoved underwater
in a bucket. Hands tied behind him. A little meet and greet
with the Magna Mater.
Divination by fruit and nuts. As for the suggestion that the BNM
     stamped on those peat

briquettes stands not for Bord na Móna
but Banca Naţională a Moldovei, that's got to be a load of
     balderdash.
It comes as no surprise the Roman goddess Pomona
oversees a cache

of linen-factory data, albeit incomplete,
written on onionskin. It turns out that Ben Hur is a patronymic
meaning "Son of White Linen." "Ben" like the "Mac" in Seosamh
     Mac Grianna,

erstwhile political prisoner. A Loyalist gunman has been known
     to yell "Trick or Treat"
as he opens fire with a semiautomatic. The dolphins continue to
     mimic
the obeisance of the dock cranes.

That's right, Lew, the obeisance of the dock cranes seems to mark another lap
of the Macedonian pirate fleet
around the Cinecittà tank. Why not fit a motion-sensitive booby trap
to the Canary Wharf bomb? A Pape had as much chance of winning a council seat

as a bird does of representing the abandoned site.
Yes, Lew, that Boston electoral district really did take the shape of a salamander.
The fact that Ben Hourihane's toga is lime-white
is emblematic of his essential candor

while the Barrett semiautomatic is seen to swivel
even as Little Miss Messala writhes
in anticipation of the amputation saw. As you drove out of Santa Fe in your gig,

Lew, it must have struck you that one way to cut through the drivel
is by welding scythes
onto the hubcaps of what was otherwise a regulation-black Humber Pig.

The pivotal point of Bloody Sunday sees a Humber Pig spinning
    its wheels
while Father Edward Daly has the Divil's
own job of escorting a dying man off the field. Many of us
    remember Whitelaw's spiel
about there being no granting of the privi-

lege of "political status" to the prisoners in Magilligan and Long
    Kesh
despite the acknowledgment of their being "special category." It
    was by dint
of becoming tribune, Lew, you became enmeshed
in mortality. I think of George Bernard Shaw's household hint

about being patient with the poor funeral attendees who snivel
because they think they ought to live forever. Maybe it's best to
    put on our purple togs
and fall in with the cavalcade

that frolics and frivols
through the streets of Jerusalem to the Isle of Dogs.
The accoutrements of empire. The opportunistic bracken's
    rusting blade.

The loathsome Squirt Pig was so named because it was fitted with
    a water cannon
before which all resistance would be shown to shrivel.
It was deployed in Dungannon
in an attempt to cut down all that civil

rights stuff about "One Man One Vote." An extra in the parade
    was brought to book
for wearing a hackle on a Balmoral
instead of a tam-o'-shanter. Pomona wields a pruning hook.
In 1959, the same year *Ben Hur* took the laurels,

Seosamh Mac Grianna suffered the loss
of his wife and son. Both committing suicide. Both throwing off
    their yokes.
Mac Grianna would spend his final thirty-one years in a
    psychiatric

hospital in Letterkenny. That's right, Lew, each of us has his cross
to bear. An explosive charge fitted to the spokes
of one wheel will as readily put paid to the Ford Cortina as the
    Roman quadriga.

The cover of An Gúm's edition of *Ben Hur* sets it firmly in the
    Third Reich.
My childhood bedroom was divided by an earthwork fosse
that connected it to the Black Pig's Dyke.
The Squirt Pig, meanwhile, was painted in Admiralty-gray
    semigloss

meant to ward off those nightscopes. Disinformation about a
    dawn swoop,
half-truths and old-style spelling errors
only partly account for the imbroglio. Little Miss Messala and his
    skiffle group
doing their best to convince the reporter for the *Daily Mirror*

(as well as the stringers for Reuters
and Associated Press) they won't succumb to the Mop Tops. Now
    the surgeon cocks
an ear to Messala's chest and checks his pulse

though everywhere the world has missed the beat. That's why
    Lonnie Donegan loiters
with the intent of cracking the combination on the lock
and seeing everything fall into place.

"My aunt Jane, she's awful smart, she bakes wee rings in an apple
    tart."
That's right, Little Miss, not only has Doctor Graves linked goiter
to a lack of iodine but he keeps on cocking his ear to the atrium
    of your heart.
The medical team is surveying you as a plow team might
    reconnoiter

a rolling mead. Try to hang in there. Don't forget how Jonah
was punished by God because he balked
at being a prophet. Some think the cult of that self-same Pomona
may be glimpsed in the apple tart. The Chiricahua leader, Victorio,
    has chalked

up so many defeats he's emerged the clear winner. The day you
    took the oath
of office was the day you found yourself trammeled.
The fiercely territorial "Apache" goshawk is the same goshawk

(*an tseabhach mór*) that was sacred to Mars and Apollo both.
As for that most disinformative call about an "apple" being made
    of "enamel,"
it's been traced to a South Armagh telephone kiosk.

That's right, Lew, when you installed yourself in the governors'
    palace
little did you think you yourself were part of the growth
and graft of empire. It's pretty clear Messala's guilty of malice
aforethought at Antioch just as it's pretty clear our children are
    still loath

to ascribe scythe-hubbed Ferraris to the Picts. Some see your
    failure to show at Shiloh
as the impulse behind *Ben Hur*. Pecs and abs, Lew, abs and pecs.
As for the idea that the bird casting its Lilo
upon the waters might be wearing an anachronistic Rolex,

that's not so much a blooper
as a timer for an improvised explosive device. The prow of the
    Havengore
continues to insinuate

itself into our consciousness. Billy the Kid lies in a stupor
while trying to grasp your offer of amnesty. Ben Hourihane is a
    lion chained to its roar.
Much as a disenfranchised Dungannon man is tied to his
    Nissen hut.

So it was that the funeral of Winston Churchill would gradually morph
into the funeral of an innocent victim of the Paratroopers.
Father Daly. His handkerchief. The innocent victims of the
    bombing of Canary Wharf.
Two kinds of grass. Regular and super.

One need only tweak the Vari-X a smidgen
to make an adjustment
in windage or elevation. A canary is also a stool pigeon,
of course, someone who sings in an English accent,

the accent reserved for the Romans. The cars in the high-speed
    chase swap
insults as they cross the border. In the way Ben was asked to rat
    on his coreligionists
you asked Billy the Kid to turn informant. It's something like a
    badge

of honor that our children spare us the details of the undercover
    cop,
tattooed glipe that he is, tied by his ankles and wrists
and staked out over an anthill in South Armagh by the Chiricahua
    Apache.

"And when Halloween comes round, fornenst that tart I'm
      always found."
The investigative team is pulling out all the stops
to establish if Mac Grianna's son committed suicide or drowned.
Because the bass player in the skiffle group has called so many
      Saturday-night hops

he manages surface tension with the grace of a common water
      strider.
It's easy to see how a UVF man posing as a B-Special
became a privileged insider.
Back in 1933, Mac Grianna had wondered if he should render
      "clockwise" as *deiseal*,

that being the direction in which a lobster (even one on a tether)
tended to move around a henge.
The British were still celebrating their victory over the
      Macedonian effetes

while every year at Navan Fort there was a hell-for-leather
chariot race in which redemption still somehow triumphed over
      revenge.
Now your bird is your wand, Lew. I'm fully aware of that.

I'm well aware that Ben Hourihane was sold cardboard shoes by
    a shoddy
millionaire from the North. Messala's hip was cobbled together
from a titanium ball-and-socket. With her bawdy
she thee warshipped, Lew, there in the nether

reaches of the *Havengore*. I'm also well aware that Judas Iscariot
doesn't play as big a role in the movie as in the book. As for the
    shtick
about the railway gauge being the width of a Roman chariot,
it was in Dungannon someone threw the half-brick

that set off the first of a line
of reinings-in of big parades. That's why it's pure chance the
    prefect would dodge
a paver or twice-baked *tegula* made of Coalisland clay.

That's right, Lew, pure chance the Mescalero girl to whom you'd
    taken a shine
would go on to dislodge
just such a tile from the roof of the governors' palace in Santa Fe.

It was in Barry's amusement park Ben had first found himself on
    a "3 Abreast Galloper"
and realized there was a fine line
between being bewildered and unfazed. That's right, Massa Lew,
    a caliper
isn't going to work. Lobsters really are a class of sea swine,

given how they grub
about in the shit. According to Sir Winston, such is the integrity
    of their limestone coral
the white-clawed crayfish love nothing better than to scrub
some data. No better place to start than with the Mescalero girl
    who refers to moral

turpitude as moral *turpentine.*
In your chest safe is the very handkerchief a nonplussed
Father Daly waved as a flag of truce on Bloody Sunday. When
    Pilate lets that hanky fall

it swerves as a morning to those who continue to wine and dine
on Massic and edible dormice, not to speak of the Seven Sleepers
    of Ephesus,
for whom this is indeed a wickiup call.

ACKNOWLEDGMENTS

Acknowledgments are due to the editors of: *The American Reader, Arts Tonight* (RTÉ), *Catamaran Literary Reader, The Guardian, Little Star, The Mimic Octopus, The Paris Review, The Penny Dreadful, Plume, PN Review, Poetry & Audience, Poetry Daily, Poetry London, The Poetry Review, Princeton Magazine, Radio Silence, TLS,* and *The Walrus.*

Several of these poems appeared in *Songs and Sonnets*, an interim collection published by Enitharmon Press in 2012. A version of "Cuthbert and the Otters" was commissioned by, and read at, the 2013 Durham Book Festival. "Pelt" was printed in a limited edition to celebrate the 2013 Folger Poetry Board Reading at the Folger Shakespeare Library. "Charles Émil Jacque: *Poultry Among Trees*" appeared in *Lines of Vision: Irish Writers on Art*, edited by Janet McLean and published by Thames & Hudson in 2014. "Pip and Magwitch" appeared in *A Mutual Friend: Poems for Charles Dickens*, edited by Peter Robinson and published by Two Rivers Press in 2012. "Rita Duffy: *Watchtower II*" appeared in *Privacy Policy: The Anthology of Surveillance Poetics*, edited by Andrew Ridker and published by Black Ocean in 2014. "Saffron" appeared in *Body of Work: Forty Years of Creative Writing at UEA*, edited by Giles Foden and published by Full Circle in 2011. "A Civil War Suite" appeared in *Lines in Long Array: A Civil War Commemoration*, published by the National Portrait Gallery (Smithsonian) in 2013. "We Love the Horse Because Its Haunch" was delivered as the 2013 Phi Beta Kappa poem at Princeton University. "Anonymous: From 'Marban and Guaire'" appeared in *The Finest Music: Early Irish Lyrics*, edited by Maurice Riordan and published by Faber and Faber in 2014. "Federico García Lorca: 'Death'" was written for the New York Public Library's 2013 celebration of Federico García Lorca's *Poet in New York*. "A Giraffe" was published in a limited edition by the Poetry Society of the United Kingdom in 2012. "Dromedaries and Dung Beetles" appeared in *1914: Poetry Remembers*, edited by Carol Ann Duffy and published by Faber and Faber in 2013. "The Firing Squad" was published in a limited edition by the University of Connecticut in 2014, while "Álvaro de Campos: '*Belfast, 1922*'" was published as a broadside by Emory University that same year. "Camille Pissarro: *Apple Picking at Eragny-sur-Epte*" was commissioned in 2013 by the Dallas Museum of Art.